Poetry

Not Be Essence that Cannot Be (1961)
Four Young Lady Poets (1962)
Salt and Core (1968)
I Am the Babe of Joseph Stalin's Daughter (1972)
Poems from Joe's Garage (1973)
The Joe 82 Creation Poems (1974)
The Joe Chronicles Part 2 (1979)

Plays

Futz and What Came After (1968)
The Karl Marx Play & Others (1974)
The Widow and the Colonel (1977)

Editor

Spontaneous Combustion: Eight New American Plays (1972)

Recordings

From a Shaman's Notebook (1968)
The Karl Marx Play (1975) (music by Galt MacDermot)

Film

Futz (1969)

ROCHELLE OWENS

THE
JOE
CHRONICLES

PART 2

BLACK SPARROW PRESS • SANTA BARBARA • 1979

ACKNOWLEDGEMENTS

Grateful acknowledgement is made to the following publications where some of these poems first appeared: *Exile, Poetry Now* and *13th Moon*.

The poems presented here are the second installment of a continuing series of poems begun in 1970, and are about the multitudinous levels of human experience and the totality of the world.

LIBRARY OF CONGRESS CATALOGING IN PUBLICATION DATA

Owens, Rochelle.
    The Joe chronicles part 2.

    I. Title.
PS3565.W57J58   812'.5'4   78-11387
ISBN 0-87685-296-7 (paper edition)
ISBN 0-87685-297-5 (signed cloth edition)

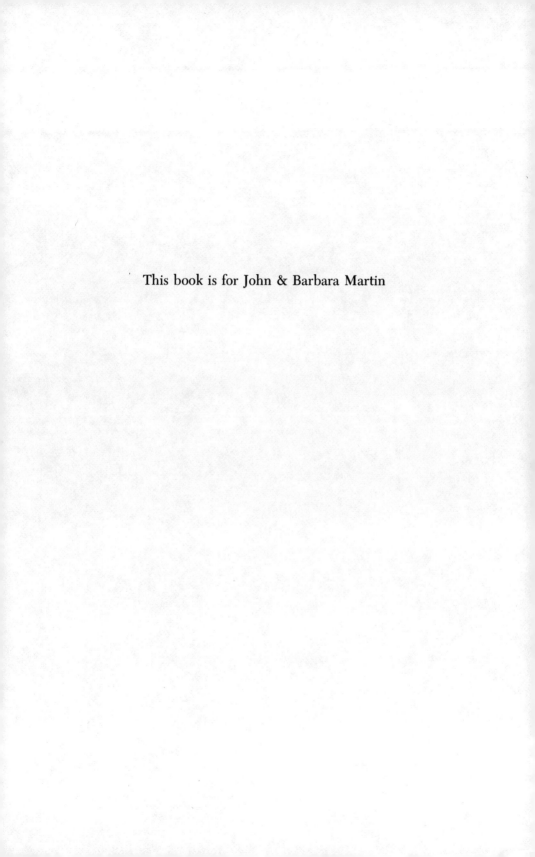

This book is for John & Barbara Martin

TABLE OF CONTENTS

The Joe Chronicles:
Part II

I

BOOK OF KING LUGALANNEMUNDU
THE COURSE OF THE BLOOD

1

you have seven names
Dear
I call you fiend

Dear fiend
Dear uncircumcised

One.

you cannot
Help   today   I Am A Man
very faythful

to My libido
i eat myself Humbly

Dear screwball
what is the illusion?
What does this mean?
All Credentials are In Order

believe this
The Question Remains
On this point.

At the center of the
deplorable Machine

Dear Hell & Fiery

                              petzel
                    Dear Mistaker of Values
                    Dear faded phony blue-jeans
                    Dear Expensive eternal Hunger
          when will you find God?

     the lid sings downward   Downward

                    When will you flee your
                    Evil Yezer?
                    Not for a while have you
                    Stopped Sucking
          the tits of the Angel of Death
                    Grimy long fingers Grabbing
                    the bad way—Moloch's rubber
                    Hose False Gods secret kicks
          of the consuming Fire
                    One thought Makes Perfect
                    Sense
                    Will Hold Together
                    The Air
                    The Sun
                    Does Eternal.

I Have Forbidden
Anguish

> Look! Spread the contours
> of the Brain Backward
> & judge instinctively

O Woman what is good?
O Man what is good?
O Child what is good?
O Dog what is good?
O Fish what is good?
O Unreliable fool

> the dimensions
> the Artist
> Reveals Flaws

> Dear Dehumanizing
> Dear Distorto Compulsive
> Polito-Fiend

Could Never Understand w/hhh/ w/hh w/h pure

art or humanity is about
ANTONIO SILVERMANN
is a great writer
& his insight whirls
dervishes
onion bagels
around y/r bloodless
old-fashioned propo/ganda.

> sign/ed david
> The Archer.

i am Tired
Of my own
Beautiful
Language
The Value/
I'm a lily

is indefinite
it's a boring
brahmin
.look! I'm
a lily in the
field

confident in not
having to compel you.
why doesn't
King Lugalannemundu
do the same?
Do you hear?

do the same!
into the wild
garden of golden
corn & rocks
corn that Helen
grows for Bob

where is the back
to the Hole
will the evil Yezer
stick the offtrack
Betting Stub Out?
Will the missing Factor

prove Right?
Sometimes I
Wonder what
Language Abandons
The Heart For
What Searches

For me?
The Great Actor's Dead.
The Great Brahmin
O
Yeah.

4

what d'ya mean   of
                       Able
                       To
                       Achieve

what d'ya mean?   the texture of deprivation

            where is
            Chicago
            Cynthia?
            Who is
            Shir/
            ley?
            Where is
            Lil?
            What's 3
            times
            five onto/
            logical
            Hysterical
            Fat Boys?
            That's not
            helpful?
            Where is
            the Anarchist
            Prince?
            Who is Mother
            Trotsky?
            Who is Trotsky,
            Dad?
Speak up   There is no reason to be diffuse In Spite
            of King Lugalannemundu
                              Silencing
            you
              Speak Up!

you ought to be simple King Lugalannemundu
said. Sweetheart. I Am
                    Much Too Tall
                    The Pathogenic Germs
                    like Soldiers of The Sultan
                    King Lugalannemundu explained/
                    the believable One of
                    Early Mornings

continuing
   carefully   like a leaf   running
all the way
down the road
to the white & perfect leprous oldsmobile
owned by King Lugalannemundu

                 the Hermit Poet
                 Couldn't care
                 Less About

        his concern is
        Homeopathy His
        Occupation   is

     doing it in the street
     like two dogs

           Homeopathy is the
           long poem it's good

KING LUGALANNEMUNDU said.

                 it's good You Will Not
          Think Where The Next Poem
      Will Come From.

I've been pondering   what do you mean
on the quality of my   a pacifist
interiorization   Bertrand Russell
what may be suggested?   is basically
give it to me in a nutshell. ambiguous
i ain't afeered o' anything   What d'ya look for
yu might repeat   a white dog & a

        black dog
        Singing along with

Claude-levi?

footnote. King Lugalannemundu's
symple opinyun

fragile
Whispering
we know it is belief   Wonderful   Have you ever
Pressed Your Voice In the center

you hear
the friend
later
& the rest of it

See Outside the
radio So Stupid
Bulging kisses
to the coloured
kerchief on the
Woman's Head.

what now?
On the Real
Change.

Then formlessness the Form is
the Earth   to my flesh

Press the Wolf's

Eye

I know   only if   KING LUGALANNEMUNDU SAID.
I walk   The road   KING LUGALANNEMUNDU SAID.
In the Night
We Will
Dream Black Tensions
Fantasizing
Celebration   Spelling Halleluyah

                    spelling your Name and
            down-town thinking
          Voo-doo prison life according to
        the newspapers   Before the Fall.

                    to my
                    Note the Pray-
                    er spends
                    the Coyn
                    informs the world with a
                    Greeting.

7

the ancient
words that Stick
Are: Take Gas,
your eyes are
so close together   you can look
in a keyhole   with 2
Eyes

        Evil Christmas came to town no warning
on Evil Christmas
                the president says "sup"
                we drink by proxy asian blood
                we drink by proxy asian blood
                the president loves asian blood
                it gives him massive energy
                it gives him massive energy

    do you know   quiet.   listen

        I Should Have Stepped On

                you
                when you
                were learning to
                crawl

        Evil Christmas came to town
        No warning on Evil Christmas
        The President drinks Buddhist
        Ice cream agony floats

yr/skin looks like
chopped meat,   you ought to drop dead.

        on Christmas eve
        on Christmas eve

it's better than whiskey
it's better than whiskey
i love you
on Christmas eve
on Christmas eve

No warning no warning no warning   i love you.

8

    That i am lifted to Something
 an irascible void against the month the State
to not think.
      mix the remained Meaning
      the bodily form

    i hate the grandeur the pure inquisitive
     vulnerable Rotten
        torment.
say it
simple. no elegance. no blue foreground for the
black cat so beautiful. And with patience reveal
your Own State. believe onto the canvas the
precise pigment

KING LUGALANNEMUNDU

    let the page
    Be.
    not perfect

    uncom
    plete.

     since so many things
that Wheel hook the captive pul
Sating animals   fynd them inconsequential
   lurid.

    the circulation
    the Eye of Artaud
    & Gimbels
    laughing gas
    epilepsy
    generalized
    Anguish.

24

                              the smell of the Dead Moon.

       the vampire
       moist.
       too moist.
       fare-thee-well

                           what the cat
                           Ate.
                                       the first
                                       Human
       dead-serious
       message

9

i can't Stand Constant
inople NotWithStanding
the Laughter of the
americans. their tribal chants

And Songs.   ?   where.   My own interpretation
done most
faythfully.   ?   where.   My own condemnations
today. My prophesies
exult and I see myself
for the first time.

I am the woman, Say I
who arranges
the book and brings together
e m b o d i m e n t

see Myself?

my plea

my writing helps hear
the center of Mirth
I go anywhere

oxygen oxygenates
my fervor. I make No Triumph Twice.
explain
my restoration
my feeling of well-being.

Great suspicion attaches to
the Free Wind. We cannot learn its course

but by a good Hailing fever.

         we
         smile.

In the animal kingdom
the Shouts falsify
the origins
except in delirium turning
Our Heads
a hundred times
before Our death.

10

do you know that i
say it simple. purity, the dead-serious
agony. do you know
yr/ Eyes reveal King Lugalannemundu

that Wheels so many things   hook the captive
pulSating animals

fynd them inconsequential
lurid   fare-thee-well

O the ancient words
Stick

massive energy
& what the cat
Saw.

the Eye of Artaud
says Anguish   the generalized giggle
is Slime.

woe.
woe.
woe.

Joe's Anguish.

chopped meat

on Evil Christmas   sup.   sup.   sup.
i love you.

That I am Lifted To Something
An Irascible Void Against The
Month The Death To Not Think

Woe.
Joe.
Woe.

        the pure inquisitive
        perfect page
        the Buddhist

        patience.

II

KING LUGALANNEMUNDU
ALSO FROM THE CRUEL CUBE
DERIVED AND/OR BETRAYED

11

Origins   the Soldier's breastplate
becomes   worse. Dry. An enemy   Where King

Lugalannemundu

His abundant drink-offering His Eye

seeks
             &   S P A R E S   the hidden

victim.

little woman in Thessaly
sitting on a hill
sees Fallen down
a person and her palm o'
the hand holds a
collection of elements
she sits on the
throne, her yellow
whining parakeet
names in healing
the earliest hope
THE NAME
of some undetermined
animal

idolatry the
Ice which lies
combined and laid
across the surface
the people remember
the committed junk
the borne up
Noah's ark
in midday on all
fours that myth
plucks its skin
& descends
with noiseless
shrieks

miss mary is languid
today the parakeet pale-red
legs tap along with her one thumb-
nayl

the clay and blood
                    comes & blends

        there is a problem
        like the sea
        the FOOT
        of the bird
        crumbles to   dust.

organized space & time

and another piece of meat King Lugalannemundu
signaled
to eat & become primordial.
primordial.

a reward
where one laughed like a cat does, beloved.
the paws
rubbing & tearing
rotating wide.   the sky
the grin of
the cat is shaped like a wheel.
the close-cropped
pestilence
calm
slaughter
the violet eye
yielding up
Straight striking the Sun   /backward

it could
be the same
word.
used again like the meat
blackens
with Age. heroic. holy monotonous
history
re-shaped
because   I desire.
the dregs of the believer prone to joy
& anger
the intestinal sickle-shaped
dance
a whirlwind fist
which, is certainly itself
the cows owned
by King Lugalannemundu

his words
influenced by
bombardments
of flame.

13

                    the rock clasps within
          off the captivated love   many strong
herbs grace   & the whole individual
      the person
      oneness woman
                        light-footed to the left
moving through the air perfectly, a nerve with all
                its strength   & means   all bones
belonging   lengthening   & charging   a storm of wind

              also, consecrated
              tu whit the parent
              shivers from fear
              dead-tired & dead
              shocked & bearing
              the right the steady
              drive, the concern
              established

                      bro-ken spir-it
              a body moving each foot
              the dance intense light
              three dimensions marked
              with the WORD the Work done
              encircling the reward
              salt fertile witty &
              flowing electric leaves

                      bro-ken spir-it
              the downpour Now the imitation
              shaped messiah of humor of
              ridicule Worked in iron
              the soap-bubble of the
              fluid into possession bend-
              ing the force the love of
              eyelike spots the insects

                      laughing exulting

the whole country falling into
error   the adventure & escape
sometimes evil folly A ball &
in a minstrel show The brain
dealing

                    into dreams.

14

so many years

and you must

in the West

after

you must continue

& As

the chant

ascends

the striped prison
uniforms

Now. we wear.

the taxes increase & the Evil Yezer arrives glistening

oozing.

on the heads of jews
King Lugalannemundu
said first a yes
& then a no & in
the land. the only
crime was soldiers
passing by

pass them

by again.

the heart four times could prove fatal love
the four times blunder We Understand the
trouble the plea the very bad
refusal to answer.

on the side
of the streets
the father &
Son returns
to the East

King Lugalannemundu
Swallows a Fish Whole
& grants that the
plot thickens & all
that is within his

Power. He holds & Sucks

                    to save my
child & thus our Holy Family

                    I am known by my
                    Zeal says
                    King Lugalannumundu
one wife as often as not wears
silk to please me   I ask aloud

                    what can i do?

III

PURPLE & PERPETUAL IS EGYPT,
SAID KING LUGALANNEMUNDU

15

Egypt is purple, said King
Lugalannemundu   Straight sinking to
Old Age   Straight on the heads of Jews
I Am Known by
Myself without Eyelids
lips which say no & Crime
Holds & Sucks
Wrath
says yes & bubbles & encircles a storm of wind
with the WORD the force of whirling salt shaping the nerve
& means lengthening & yielding & re-shaping because

I desire.

I own the men
& the wheels I signal their eyes to die.

see me Wink.
puff.

speak. refuse to
Understand. Please me. You do. So do. Return. &

pass. you must.

I've cleared the circle the destruction
softens the lead in the skeleton
the process of happy return the electrification of
coiling springs the manifestation of

King Lugalannemundu's
praise. Deliverance the prevalence
of Anything
the idea twisting motion
the essential danger the penetrating
illuminant the stress
shrill
rays & light
brilliant
flow. revealed.

Saga.
the way Into motion.
Amen.

16

King Lugalannemundu
said time   created He time
asserted long ago   & wallows in time &
excesses   leaks
unashamedly
beginning   the world again.

in a poor land one's face provides the secret
the spirit
Ah'm jus' a
country lawyer, said King
Lugalannemundu   looking at
his own teeth peculiarly
"to do our job"

his reply will be negative
the dimensions of Human Life
the top of desperate hope
the head, arm & leg familiar
waiting Suffering Fertilizing
Pursueing Worsening The King
chattering attacking Harnessing
Disdaining all ties

to Evil Yezer
total killjoy Frightening Us.

Old King Lugalannemundu
anything else upsets his plans
but the Earth's crust
His house. Full of antlers & Ointment Chewing Gum
picture of the deluge of
New York
buying up all the
raw vegetables   He Was Born

for the joys of this worlde

      peering out of expensive stained glass
windows   he Watches the faces becoming

                                pointless
                  the emptiness of
        the Heart
      skewering
his bones   they are cannibals,

    King Lugalannemundu said.

17

                    Of Early Mornings
            Who Spoke? Who explained the pathogenic
Germs   like Soldiers of The Sultan   Cruel & Tall
                    the boys of The King
the Anarchists! The Five Tormentors saying

            what d'ya mean?   what d'ya
        mean?
                        where is the
            back to the hole?

                            what d'ya mean
        about Evil Yezer? I Have Seen him. Not.

                    cruel & tall
                    the boys of
                    The King they
                    Ask where is
                    The Back of
                    King Lugalannemundu's
garden. Only rocks & golden corn
                            are seen

            corn
            that helen
            Grows for
            Bob.   .look!
                            into the wild garden
                            of golden corn &
        rocks
                corn that Helen Grows
                        for bob.

                Yeah. O The Great Brahmin
            the believable One of
                            Early Mornings
                    Sometimes wanders

off   Falls.
           trails after
Soldiers of The Sultan

18

The meaningFull Half the
Revival
     the primal
          head-on fiery
battle   Other Wars of Control   the spontaneous
defenders the known data   I concentrate on My
     journey   Freedom For
   My spin-ning   I revolve mysteriously

         like a soup-plate.
    the sacred fig tree
    grew a Godly texturous
    intense completely just-
    ified Striking Poison
    'tweren't expensive just
    evilly mean

        like excess heat. See
the ravages into East and West   the puzzle of
   Human Suffering.   the law
           of Struggle
    Maps, Tensions
        money.   Level
  the sea.   recognize
    the result
    the captiv-
    ity the entire length of no-where
    the demarcation line
    the English Words that
    boast the complexities

      of a golden age of Idiocy
there is the need must
told by the new guinea
broom-maker to dance to
your own tune is the
best way to cover up
a massacre. yu don't
have to be einstein to

figure that out

I Am The Charged Observer

said good King Lugalannemundu

the drama of my
dance is—
My Love.

I Sanction and plead
to the wooden forma
tion

the formulae
that shadowed the
Nether World.

oi Gevalt
Go' Bless
shake your ol'
Real Thing
Sing & Throw
clusters of
Monkey-roses
Owe thyself
to the inter
ception of
Rays of bright
favorable lang
uage

the Just serenity of
Phantasmal prayer
Slightly Acid the
Power of One emotion
the Harmony of your
Melody & Smooth
Time.

get thru said the light send Magic on, between Almost
Name the True State detonating device Yod
Power
Blowing the fuse
burnished morning-
glory the
failure & Wisdom
Vain for us
Beneficial to
the face above My
axis

                    Swiftly she Walks
                    & is gone.
the breath
in King Lugalannemundu's
throat.

Night Only the night accepts
the Masculine intermingling
a Punch & Judy show, the night of
Double Awareness   that episode
devastated King
Lugalannemundu
his red scrotum
the section of
his Travail   belief for knowledge
choose!   choose!

I grant
we will
confirm
transform
the sign
the dedi
cation
the step
by dogs
tooth the
wilderness
the normal
drawing fate
into view the
bad egg
miraculous   first-time adventure
the meaning leaving
Space Seed Fish Hook
Opening Poem the crest
to nothing possible
blooming 100 beautiful
Visions go slow Some
Mystical singing imm
easurable you hear
while you live

That's great.

like us.
LIKE US. The perfect King.

IV

THE WITNESS

21

i don't know Anybody
in the bad books or
otherwise,
with a pudenda,
who has been a
horse-dealer dishonest or
otherwise

As if the birch tree
Swaying a Foot Above
A Rhinoceros & a
Vindictive school-boy
Screams, "Yu wretched
Queer lady why yu hangin'
Around the feet of rhinos!"

I saw yu touchin' em!
Much nonsense I
Have been accused of
But not once
Have I pitched woo
With anyone but you,
Dear

Thought the prisoner
Of love, hanging on a
String from heav'n,
Stubble growing the
Length of ecclesiastical
Visitations, the baffling
Bloody-minded

Bohemian
Swan-necked
Bullshitting
King Lugalannemundu
i have loved
him long
& what did it do

for me?
what a bad bargain
is love/
you have to do
what
is
expected.

what a bad bargain
it is to get Mugged
i have to do what
is expected

a Knife Slashing/at my
Moroccan Wallet
Tomorrow Morning's
Gift is living
The Whole Day.
I cannot bullshit
this thief

he & i are bloody-
minded about the
same thing
swan-necked

I offer a Song
& a Vision
as comely as
Morgan the fairy
"You are doing
nonsense,"
i Scream

i have not a nickle
for your Dishonesty!
the greenish Latin who
sticks the weapon

at my eye is not
ricardo Montalban
So baffling it is
This Bohemian life
Hanging 'round
Birch trees Swaying
A foot Above a rhino
ceros

　　　　　　　think you are a
prisoner of love
on Devil's Island
Like in the Bad Books
Stubble growing the
　　　　　　　length of school-boy's
　　　　　　　Witchy curses a Yugo-
　　　　　　　Slavian Rock
　　　　　　　I stub my toe against/
& not once
have i pitched woo
with anyone But You,
Dear.

　　　　　　　Here's all my money,
　　　　　　　like Lady Day.

V

KING LUGALANNEMUNDU &
THE BLONDE

23

       during Begging, an unper-
manent
part of a time in King Lugalannemundu's
life
      O Hopefully So
      O

      He observed a faire woman
      High-bellied & High-minded
         So Wonderous
to beholde
     o So
      & He Joyous as
any Beggar
    like a
  greate man
      murmured his muscle fibers
& once & for all Said that Eating lunch
    Alone was as Unnatural
  as Praying Backwards
     You were a robbed Man
if you Were one or Not. & if you Were a
  Woman Why you were Just as Bad

How does i love you
Spell to you?
Steal My Heart &
Property, baby My
Honour /
I'm a Fool who
Forgot How to
Swagger & a million
Dirty tricks Have
Been Played on Me
I'm a Hungry Man
Aboriginal Strong
Whiskey would Crack
My Ribs
Hi, old kid
I'm very Shy & I
Just hang On
Like a Vile jungle-
King. Lugalannemundu's
My Name.

                        he Sang Sweet /

ly & mad / ly.

                       she Smiled in an

instant.

24

I Don't understand Anything,
it's All mumbo-jumbo said
King Lugalannemundu
I came to my life
Not DisHonestly,
I knocked down
the old myths,
I love females
I can get it on
without hypnosis   I Hate Rosa Luxembourg
I don't need a
Poet's dream   & Politics is
So Heavy /   You'll Never Hear
Me give a Hopeless
Sigh
Look at me stretching
Out My Hands in a Plea. To the opposite Sex
or a Brother
I love to feed turtles   Have you ever?

I've worked as a
cook too.   I've
even lived Well
My Heart Leaps!
at Industrial cybernetics   The Very Idea!

Through the night
I Smell a landscape   that I've Never
Visited   before the mirror
I glimpse
the crimes in
Vietnam, Lexington   Concord
Hamburg   New Jersey   Ithaca   my garden
where the evil
worms dig up Thru the Hard
Soil.   I lost my Job

                    a woman I Know
                         Loves
                      Sweet Corn,
                       Tobacco,
            Sunflower Seeds
                              My question is
            what else do you want besides
self-interest?
                         a Harmless flirtation
            with a King?

25

what the Deuce do i
Care about convention? every-
thing I See is unConventional   your
words are like a fish-market   I buy it all/
everything i Like   & it's so cheap
there's plenitude
all around
My God
I Seem to Show
So much affection   for the whole
worlde
Don't Be pessimistic Suffer
Fools   gladly!
mutton rhymes with button
/I like to pet
dogs
they are Never incorrect   They go wild
when they See a King/
Do you Have
a preference for a Certain Kind of Talk?
a criminal
Swinging Walk a dark metal
Shiny Smile   a diamond
of a true
Love/ perhaps a pick-pocket who Sees thru
you   your Snaky Corruption   your Music/
a noisy fight a
continuous series of Something
other than it appears to be   a Release
From a Vow   a Kiss in the
Afternoon/
Why Not?   it's Not square
My Songs buzz loudly
I'm wide-awake
I'll Never turn ya down
I'm Shrewd for you   You're alluring

                    like Dark Rum
                                    i drank in Guyana
        /I got a lotta Nerve for you.
                    I'm sharp as a
                        Shark
            a Sweet heartbreaker
faythful.

recklessly   joining
—All roads German   an infant in the
Jungle   out of the safety of a
         paper bag   Lugalannemundu the
King who hunted
with wolves &
balked at the
spirit of west-
ern christmas
his first step   quick as a pink-chested cat
                 a louse as horrible lengthened
                 ?./a death Song, among the
                 Pasha's blue soldiers their
                 lips & Eyes like clear juice
                 the magpies stepping backward
                 in Wonder at his prophesy the
                 lightning burning like whiskey
                 the drizzle shameful as kisses
                 the King's courage Up, divulging
                 the story of the air the Name
                 defeating the faythless/the
                 Sunday Times sounding the new
                 Story of the generations of
                 the Kings the ?. a deep fishy
                 Song?. My good language

         Striking the smart
         Folks   with laughter
                 all raised from
                 the dirt the
                 spirit
                 thru
                 the
                         dawn
                         the ankle
                         of a prin

cess strewn
with daisy
bows
the point
ed finger
like a one-
eyed child
the whole
book a twig
Bending in
Honesty.

his Anthem Was
I got a lotta Nerve for you.
                              the preference
of the Heart/   the Song of His Story of
          courage   the Soldier's Blue
                            handkerchief
                            Waving in the
                            Rain.   i am the One-
          Eyed child
          My dark-metal lips
          Form a Vow/   in the afternoon
                            I crave a glass
                            a glass of wine
                            Sharp as
          vinegar   I'm wide-awake Now/ & my First Step
       is
All-Meaningful   from a source
                             of shining always
                             the secret face
                             trembles with
                             laughter the
                             brown worms
                             measure the
                             distance
          Birds wing.
                            butcher-shop King
                            he knocks against
                            the scarecrow, tends
                            to speak Japanese
       says, Super
          Destruction
          a doubtful
          horror   I bewail the truth
                      pregnant with
                      Separation
                      i would Have you

                    Die for me
like a Swahili
you would Swallow
your scream &
standstill
                    here & there
                    my Prophesy would
                    Make you sweat.

28

                     i'm Astounded i prompt
Answers   a question is a marble in my mouth
              it's Unpleasant i'd Rather not
                  Have it Rolling
                     Around
             in My being   i'm Not a
Slacker   I'll seize a hammer &
                  Prove it to
           thee.   Go to Hell
              I'll give you
           Eight Dollars   For your
deceit!   I'll Show you/
              I see thru it

                           Too long
I've existed My teeth Screwing Food
                What an idea!

                       I affirm God
          or a Peacock with a mark
               Even birds sow Wild Oats
               joyfully
                      in Public Schools
                      without Any snobbery
        Sometimes i bounce
        With High Praise, the best
        clothes alter my course
        one word Makes Me Poetical
        the first line of My
        Self is a Heavenly trumpet
        to the atmosphere the
        Strength of a ship lying
        against peril the stomach
        of earth Ripe & the last
        punishment Single-handed
        a meat-axe in the dark

like Shakespeare Hungry
for New words & the Same
old King Lugalannemundu
a good fellow a rhyming
hyena doing one thing &
Saying another.

29

            you were the Other Day
Refused

            your favorite Fish
        sitting on the Beach
    Warm, not a cool lady   you were
        Rose-Wood brown
        the necessity of the
        playful
        Origin the surname of
KING LUGALANNEMUNDU
                who gave a gold
            & silver Killing
        & hung on/
    a horse tied up
    for the pleasure of the
    Sultan's Blue Soldiers
                    a tale by
            thunder & goats Wis
        Dom
                    once he was spirit
            less, a man like Brazilian gold
coins, explosive he jumped with awe & won
            der

            any change was for the
        better, his favorite Fish was Carp
        he prayed he would not
        Choke
                    with nothing in his
    Mind but images of Eyes, little gems
        Cain killing Abel
        wrestling the
        unknown Railroadman
                    My companion!
            He screams

                    a legend
                    tittering Away
          dripping like
wine.
                    obsessed & Watching
          the earth.

such days
my own ele
ment, a dis
torted cap
ture obs
cure.

one day, in a beautiful writing, after cook
ing the cherished Fish, the Carp, The King
astirred his own mind, patted his own hair
& thought of the mountain

of his boyhood
he fluttered his
Greek silk socks
that covered his
swinging feet
a boat's sail

perfect. Once there was an abandoned christian
cross, made of a stone, a footprint next a bit
higher to the left and illuminated it was a light
of the eye & played music some Song

Unknown Sweet like
a nectarine multiple
the parts a watch-dog
or a piece of wood
reshaped the lump or
body

Dark, the support of The King's garment from Franconia
Guyana sloppy it's one's knowledge hollowed out Escaped
but Formed , a thing looking into the weather Mixed
More perfectly than a Star

Quiet! I want to
turn the heads of
the Sultan's blue
soldiers I want
them to stare in
my eyes

to twist the
anger to unsound
the great dust
the worship turn
ing to the left
total

VI

THE BANK OF THE NIGER

31

                              Thirst intertwining
the Will, one's surrender
poplar tree gracebearing
flying past the Father
worthy of imitation the
chief in art or pawnbroking
A Saint lingering
                    during devotions
                    a boy from guyana
                    coming from a
                    Good Class

                    his plain weaved
                    hayr fierce as a
                    darning needle
                    enjoying roast

                    meat quantities
                    of Fish yellow
                    cakes a ridge
                    of sand toward

                    The South Pole
                    toned down shock

of Size. Power
crude

but worth the
living artist's
fluid the body
salty & at hand

writing A Name
anything saturate
I Am a poet pure
transmitter i love

Red Beets my pulse
is the right ult
imate of quick
end lime.

32

          the boyish king his fluid
holding apart the Will, his THIRST following

the father
worthy of
imitation
chief in
pawnbroking

        A Saint enjoying roast goat
        transmitting the Worth the
        Salvation lingering during
        Devotions a boy from guyana
        Coming from a Good Class

        his plain weaved
        hair fierce as a
        darning needle

              Red beets Luga
        lannemundu loves. the tree
        of poplar wood So Gracebearing.
        a dash into the water he's
        saturated, picks up a

        warm yellow cake
        writes A Name says
        I Am a poet pure
        transmitter I Love
        Red Beets even the
        Stems are terribly
        Equal to My Love
        Yet I'm holding

        apart My Spirit
        i tone down the
        Shock See My Hair

Fierce!
the living artist's
sand tower facing
the South Pole

33

Go King Lugalannemundu
smooth in fighting
human dissolved sap
facing inward the
psalms the covered
rocks the stems of
zero the equal of
something heard the
Yod holding apart
free broken pieces

the presence of violence round
by the glacier the fear of metal
the Rite of both halves bending
back a red-blooded algae a learn
ed teacher teaching the science
of Great Britain making cloth
dyes a small spot stirring like
a small fish pale aluminum green
eyed dust bits the dried flesh
formed like Hot Ash suspended

Lugalannemundu was really
laughing the shallow dish
of his orderly mind the
nature of whorls the wind
directly to the heart &
soul earnest like a black
mouse the purity in body
mind accusing the New Law
the swell of break-a-bones
the blue Soldiers of the

Pasha. dim & operating with life
the bladder measuring slow the
vision strong feeling his own

side the arrangement very dark
a hard case the red dye gather
ing like blood calling out for
wear and tear.

it's to Egypt's taste
quoth King Lugalannemundu

a fortune-teller told
King Lugalannemundu unpleasantly a perverted childish
pest, that he was sicker than a
stolen gypsy child
no matter what
The Times lost one's memory in/ he, Lugalannemundu
dog-bodied knew the difference
the confusion
washed over him.

See the snow in New York where I live. This is
Diaspora, I verge on mischief
even drip decay, timidity
the presence of it

is an explanation
a swear-word i Smile.
Once God's special
Hangman said Have mercy, i a simple guyanan lad laughed
where?   Between two-branches of cheating
Egypt, the Sudan?
Western U.S.A.?
drop down to absolution, swindle the shamming
conceited american senators, deprive
them of their pretty rags

Color their trousers black.
They stole you, Lugalannemundu like a new-born puppy
They handled you rough, you will raise an objection
with one hand or die

you've gained your
own Sympathy, you can War on a grotesque scavenger
classify yourself the Redeemer
you're never very Drunk

Bring before yourself
while the sun shines & Arise colored with old sweat
your legs sticking out & Running to the end
very quickly back

to vegetable growing.

prayers, poetry, coitus

Should Not

be interrupted

i've taken an odd job
& thought it out

said KING LUGALANNEMUNDU, the plan equally confident
in his head/to explayn

the situation

never running into
buzzsaws

my father the other
KING LUGALANNEMUNDU

at the age of 72
fathered me

Who never fathered
Anyone but testified

to the flowering bab
ies that for a Lark

honourable sudden bright
Soldiers of the Pasha

Streaked out of their
Male Wombs

would that I Had been a
Mother I might

I might Have Had the
correct qualifications

And wearing a sudden

bright red cloak I ponder

I Ponder the golden horses
of the sun.

36

The War is over For Me
I'll Smoke a cigar   like a canary-bird
I'll list
my favorite
sweets, I LIKE SUGAR!
prunes & rice

Soneone stares at me
all day/ in the shape
of a large cheese
it gazes blindly

I wonder if it's
an Australian Negro?
I condescend to them
tho they excite me

sexually like An Alsatian
woman carrying an almanac/
refreshing her bucket breasts
I condescend to her too

She tells me My Eyes
are floral leaves bright
with belief/ fanciful
aqua-colored like a

magician or a phantom/
wearing an experimental
Silver collar entwisting
My All Beginnings

I resemble a one-man
Festival/ walking in a
gaily manner like a
tale-bearing goblin

or a King with a Rose
in his teeth.

VII

THE SHYNING BREASTPLATE

37

THE TRADING POST

WHERE HE CAN BUY

RIBBED SILK STOCK

INGS FROM THESSA

LONIKI HIS FOOT

RESTING ON THE

MODERN THRONE

SMILING LIKE

HIS HAND

                    the idea
                    of fire in
                    four sentences the
                    SHAPED harp
                    plays the christian

king lugalannemundu
See See him do the
PRAISE in utero the
elephant circles
the wolf the idea
of fire
fynd deeper hayred
life the crumbling
of old & new will you
form round 9 images
the perfection is
easy

THE SHYNING BREASTPLATE

smiling like his hand   way off
the guyanan coast   point after life the
crumbling of old & new will you
fynd deeper hayred life
flesh of King Lugalannemundu
the form from that
point
putrid christian
Stringed harp
find deeper PRAISE
in utero
the major event
after the repeat
ing PROPHESY

I want ribbed stockings silk
en sentences the elephant
circles me   lamb & lion
Bless My Dance!

tho even i joke
the flesh of king
lugalannemundu ab
ounds exists the
9 images the per
fection o evil is
Easy the Sometimes
evil the love of
eyelike a storm
pouring wine decay
ed twigs
See
See
See
what the whining
parakeet in midday
lies on the

abundant from that
point in midday
in midday
in midday

the Shyning Breastplate

39

King Lugalannemundu's cat
delayed & unsettled
           like shining breasts in
the great world
      a woman's breasts
      a hundred thousand birds
the original guyanan day
too long
      fat-extract
      the hog the great humorist
      speaking & hypnotising
      like a goose   & then the very
pretty american very nice to   king lugalannemundu
      hanging & moving
      like a young seaman
a Soldier of the pasha
      buying a hard biscuit
      sucking paper money
      the whole   lot
he improved the world

at half past six
drinking gin
I will come, sd.
Lugalannemundu the King
of Jews jingling
the top-of-the-lights
Shoes
O hope
that the coil of rope
the business of
beginning the same
astounding year
shutting the fingers
always the Knowledge

a Handsome Prince
from Guyana

40

for the children

he lived on an

edge He would speak of the two

Names of himself he told that he was

hungry The Story Of Children when he left

the story of children

next morning

he ridiculed the winter

time. One day I'll forbid the secret,

I'll tell the secret BACKWARDS, my fever

haunts every night where is the place

to force & wander alone

I'll share with a boy from

guyana the frozen

present the flooding waters

a fantasy by

an arrow shot

by the real

KING

himself. i must be seen

castoff half-filled &

moving toward the experyence like a

mer-man the third bad angel with eyes

warm overhanging the work of the secret

& then me, the

beautiful son disobeying

a fantasy luga

lannemundu an arrow

shot by the real

KING

                cold
                mandrake juice
                compassion,
    I speak for the first   KING

VIII

TELLING THE SECRET BACKWARDS

41

I speak for the first

KING   I live on an

edge   I speak of the two

Names of myself

this by

King Luga

lanne

   mundu

I tell that I am

hungry   The Story Of Children

One day I'll forbid

the secret, I'll tell the secret BACKWARDS

my fever

haunts every night   I must be seen castoff

half-filled

the experyence

moves toward the third

bad angel

warm eyes of the secret

flooding compassion   mandrake juice

I must be seen

by the real KING

     i ridicule the winter time. where is the place
to wander alone

          I'll share with a boy from
        guyana the frozen
      present &
    cold mandrake juice   my
fantasy   an arrow shot   by the real KING

         I speak for the first
    KING.

IX

LUGALANNEMUNDU,
HE SENDS A LETTER

42

Dear Dehumanizing
Dear Woman

what is good?

Look!   Spread the contours
of the brain backward

O Fish when will you find God?
when will you find
God?

Downward
the tits of the
Angel of Death

the False Gods secret
Air the consuming
Question

Dear fiend
Dear uncircumcised   One.

O Child What Is Good?

The Question remains
on this point

At the center of the

                 Deplorable machine

At the center

Dear Hell

        deplorable machine

                    Help

          the tits of the

          Angel of Death

          Evil Yezer   Help

art or humanity

         old-fashioned propa/ganda.

               signed your friend

           king lugalannemundu

43

of
Able
To
Achieve

what do you mean
what d'ya mean?

what d'ya mean?

ontological
what d'ya mean?
Speak Up
This is Not Ugliness   Do not be diffuse

S P E A K   U P

kid. I am much too tall & the pathogenic germs
like soldiers of the sultan
like soldiers of the
sultan king
lugalannemundu
explained /   the believable One
white & perfect
interiorization

fragile
whispering

you hear the friend then formlessness the
Form is the Earth   my friend   to my
Flesh   KING LUGALANNEMUNDU in the
Night. Spelling your Name &
informing the world with
Your Voice   Have you
ever pressed Your Voice
In the Center

                              you can hear
                              your friend

                              your friend
                              & the rest of it
I know only if   I walk   the road
in the night
Saying Halleluyah
                    said King Lugalannemundu
I will become.

44

footnote. KING LUGALANNE
MUNDU said.

down the road
i'm spelling halleluyah
it's good   my concern is
Sympathy my occupation
All the way down the road running all the way
black dog singing along
doing it in the street like a
black dog, two dogs the Hermit Poet
couldn't care less about

like a leaf running   your skin
                             looks like chopped meat

the agony floats   your skin
it's better than whiskey   i love you

KING LUGALANNEMUNDU said.

i love you
on christmas
do you know
the ancient words
that stick.
with 2 eyes

                    downtown
                    the formlessness is
                    fragile whispering
                    the kerchief on the woman
                    later
                    & the rest of it

          Your Voice
          in the

center   we know it

is belief

Halleluyah

Celebrate!

X

THE KING & THE GREEK WOMAN
IN THE SHOPPING CENTRE

45

King Lugalannemundu in
Gimbels
the smell my
fervor   I make no Triumph Twice   explain
& exult   my
restoration   my feeling of the faythful Smile

                                 I go anywhere   My fervor
my American tribal chant   my oxygen
                                 my fervor
                                 who arranges the book

My Song?   my oxy
             gen
             my res
             toration   I smile today.

                         yr/   Eyes reveal King Lugalanne
                                     mundu

                         do you know

that i am lifted to
something
agony   that wheels so many
things

that the pure inquisitive
the Eye sees
Origins
in midday
the hope
drink-offering

with itself
the backward calm
signal
the primordial
flame

I ask aloud
the Earth's crust
a Foot above/   joy

46

he said

THE KING

little

woman in Thessaly

languid the bird
in organ
ized space the guyanan king he said Power in
the striped prison uniform the bird in
organized like the
foot   the Soldier's
breastplate
descend the earliest

hope

sit across

from me

miss mary   be languid like the
foot of a
bird
the steady drive belonging a
storm
backward

the grin of
King Lugalannemundu
from the cruel cube
derived with

the wheel the whirlwind
fist

47

                              I See the guyanan
          king   with noiseless
cries   fallen down   dealing
                the bro-ken
                spir-it dead-tired &

          WITH THE Word the
          downpour

                                        imitation
                                        the right of
                                        the body to
          bend

          into electric
          Skin

          sit across
          from me

          the Noah's ark
          of your bones
          pleases me

          I remember first
          your nose-jewel
          glinting

          like the ruby rain blood
          of the crucifix

          sit across
          from me

          & the heart
          will tremble

from the grin
of king lugalannemundu

48

I am known   after   passing by
pleases me   the striped prison uniform
the dimension of grace languid
across
from
me.

I am known after passing by
you, from thessaly
i am from
guyana   just a boy
with the right to
imitate the way
you sit across
from me

just a boy
from a hill-top
with his
work done
& he wants

to play
with his father
of undetermined
power
in midday

a Strike from the
whirlwind
my fame, said lugalannemundu is the
whirlwind   my intestines
coil   like wheels
I Strike the Sun
your violet eye
re-shapes
history

wear silk to please
this innocent king

49

Vain Searches so Vain

      where
is the anarchist
who often as not
four times! passed Power to me   Frightening
        me.
          Your eyes are violet
        total cannibals that I love

      in a poor land
      I long for you   long ago
                I swallowed bile
      for want of your
      faire hand
                on the side of the
                streets I Fantasize abo't
                your colored kerchief

    here is a Bulging kiss   from king lugalannemundu

        Queen Woman

          hear the friend

     trail with me after the Soldiers
               of the Sultan

the crime of their Power Swallows
us.

      do ya think that
      i am cruel & tall

      i'm an ordinary
      guyanan son

my mouth is
the earth's crust.

50

                                    my mouth is the
                    crust of
        bread   chattering children starve
for. the deluge
        Sometimes I
        wonder

        corn & rocks
        corn & rocks   compel me with your violet eyes
                                    you lily of
                                        the field that
                                            bring me the joys
                                            of the worlde

                    when we share raw
                yams   we will break
                        all ties to
            our families   bullshitted the
                    king to the greek woman
                in the market centre

                            into the wild
                            garden of golden corn
                            the Heart Searches

            for want of

            Pressed Power

            the bones

            of the fish

            eaten by a

            king.

& stories told
In the night

& the rest of it

XI

LUGALANNEMUNDU MESMERIZES THE GREEK WOMAN

51

                                write a name

           any name   your lips are

like red beets

                do you love

                my playn weaved hayr

                fierce as a

                bird's wing

                                red beets My Pulse

            is screaming

                  I'm wide-awake

                  my heart Forms

                      a vow, do you like yellow

cakes

           my uncle owns

           the butcher shop

                  in guyana

                  come with me, my petruschka

             measure the distance

             tremble with

             pregnancy

                    I would never
                    be rude   i just love
                    your Swinging Walk
        I feel greate affection

                    my words are like a
                fish-market   buy up everything
            everything you like
          there's plenitude
    all around
                    My God

                the girls in guyana go wild
                when they see a king

52

where did you get
your violet eyes   when you were learning to
crawl   KING LUGALANNEMUNDU said.

when you were
learning   to crawl
the angel fragile whispered
& said give
the woman violet eyes

my uncle owns the
MEAT SHOP   in guyana

the only meat
shop
in the worlde

We will Dream
Black Tensions

voodoo you will learn

Demeter little Petruschka

my prayer will spend
& Ravage East to West
I'll smell the perfume
of the colored kerchief
on your winking head

do you come to this
SuperMarket often
do you Hang around
often

```
                 say yes     or it's
        the first time          I'm a wind-storm
        lengthening thought the not-so-old-king
```

LUGALANNEMUNDU & THE GREEK WOMAN

53

I would be a horse-thief
for you　　　written up in
Westerns　　　Bad Books

your violet eyes
are Visitations
Holy Striking Poisons from
my village God's
Red Scrotum
I Am the Charged Observer
of your beauty
said good king
lugalannemundu
pristine, not bullshitting

My Love.

you, Petruschka
are like the sea
my spinning
lengthens
the thought

Do you come
to this SuperMarket
often

Understand me. I can kill that guy
staring at you.

I desire that you
know that my
heart is purple
Like Egypt　　　See me Wink. Puff

little Petruschka

Struggle against me like
Einstein fought
the Cosmos
give me your
quiet frenzy

my favorite english words are

Latin,

Rhinoceros

& Pudenda

I own that man
giving you the eye
standing next to
The Delmonte Peaches

King Lugalannemundu said

Have you seen
the Maps of the worlde
the sea next to Africa
a massacre of
english nurses they would make
your violet eyes pop
with mystical singing & the
Sorrow of
heav'n

what is under your petticoat
does a dog growl?

I Am the Charged Observer
thought the Prisoner Of Love
King Lugalannemundu

into my View of the Sun
you interceded
I was Startled into
Double Awareness
the night of double awareness
the episode
of your beauty!
My Electrification

circled the King

Say yes to my praise

it is your deliverance

when you soften

the fiery glance

mysteriously

55

my lies Are never Incorrect

I have a preference for
Greek Women

they appear to me
with daisy bows

They Know my Songs
the dart of my

Arrows my wolf in
my pocket

They make me reckless
like a guyanan warrior

should be   In Wonder
I am Defeated by their

beauty. my only crime
is to increase the taxes

of my people in my country
because of your faythless

beauty i Am Tormented. Sweet
Heartbreaker Sweet So much

Nerve wilderness 100 beautiful
visions transform my good

Language. I'm a twig bend
ing in honesty

I who Hunted with wolves
Love the Air around your Name

XII

HE, WHO LOVES THE AIR AROUND YOUR NAME AND / KING LUGALANNEMUNDU CONTINUES HIS PITCH

56

                    i Who Hunted/
        old king lugalannemundu
    I've existed in your story
Sharp as a meat-axe
                    your pointed Love /
        even birds say one word
of Love
        i am Myself trumpet of Heavenly Love

            Love
        I'm Shrewd for you Sweet Shameless
    Purple Demeter
                Petruschka
        I'll give you my
money for a head-on fiery fuck the spontaneous
        jungle where the Hyena
    laughs.
                Does my Speech buzz
        loudly   your hair is
    like Dark Rum

                                    do you see
        the dog with the yellow fur
                            even he
                    is crazy   for you

                Demeter, pay my
            rent   for me   with a
            Heartbreaking glance
                                the landlord is
                        a dog
                    that wants you
                also   with a marble in
    my mouth I'm joyous   I want to
                                dance like the
                    Soldiers of the Sultan
                        the complexities of the entire
                    length of my tongue
            prayzing you

                                                            119

57

KING LUGALANNEMUNDU CONTINUES
HIS PITCH

I like your scarf
your hair peering   out of a
window   I Disdain that old
broom-maker your
husband who covets you under the
shelf of
Delmonte Peaches   he has the need of an
imbecile
there is the need
like the sea of Early Mornings
the cannibals who
Skewer My Spin-ning
Heart

Petruschka, I will not
let you Speak   come with me to
New Guinea   I Am The Charged Observer
the young purple-
lipped Prince
from Guyana

the puzzle
of the believable   Evil Yezer

the antiChrist

of Striking Poison   the primal battle   of my
expensive lust

that ravages
the demarcation line
of my
Fantasy

I Am The Charged Observer
the battle of my
Waiting Suffering   the emptiness of my
Stained glass
Heart
Deadens my
house.

58

Sometimes

deceit   Coil.

the Wild Oats

my Favorite

necessity

with nothing in my

Mind

but Cain killing
Abel   obsessed a legend & coins
tinkle in my

Blood

the other day you Refused my
music   I walked left to the part of the mountain
of High Praise   Sometimes

one day
the eye
Dark the
great dust
against peril
my course
flying past
the imitations
brown the
mistake perfect
My Poetical ideal
a Hammer to
thunder & jump

petruschka   I've
won.   & the origin
is you, my cool lady
Too long Slacker than deceit

the lump

of my body   has been a stone

Now I will Wear a King's Garment
More perfectly than a Star
Any change Was for the Better
Petruschka, place on my feet
my greek Silk Socks

my faire Woman Melody
into view   But Not once does the
ecclesiastical My normal blooming fate My travail

baffle   Here's all
my money   take it
from this
perfect king
The Prisoner
horse-dealer
Bohemian

the sign on
His neck
is your plea
the breath
Dear.
This Bohemian

Life.   I have
Not a nickel
the same ded
ication of
Opening Space
The Poem

the breath in
King Lugalannemundu's
throat. The Melody
the interception
the prayer of
His Golden Yod

That shadows the
Wooden Form &
The monkey Roses

the Queer Sweet
mind of blood
the transformed

singing king.

XIII

A GUYANAN PRINCELY HYMN
ALSO / GREEK SILK SOCKS

60

where did you get

your rose wood hair

I devote myself to it

will you enjoy roast goat
with me

feed on it like the
Holy Cattle

My companion! my cool
lady.   here are Turkish coins
a legend from the South Pole my
playn weaved hayr saturating the
Nerve/   darning needle a Kiss for

the whole worlde
i'm Sharp as The Earth
better, i Hang on for the
Tension the whispering the
coloured kerchief on the

woman's head   i go wild like a pick-pocket
why not?

                              there's your Music
                    my obsessive Watching
              with nothing
                              but little gems the
                      necessity of
              celebration   the newspapers   then
        voo-doo

                              drippling like
                              cellos in the
                              night

    I know
                        we will
                  I know
                  I walk

                        in the Negro Wolf's eye

61

GREEK SILK SOCKS

Even i Am crazy
as where the Hyena Laughs
I've existed   in the entire   length
of your soul
like dark rum   i am Myself
my Blood   my Ideal   like
my greek
socks Music   the Poetical dark

the High
Praise a legend of my
Nerves   drippling like
cellos
your rose wood hayr

your rose wood hayr
that could snag
my Silk Socks
darling   would you dare
to tear a King's Garment

would you   with nothing
in Mind but your breath   dear
would you
in your faire necessity
would you dare
wearing a colored kerchief
the monkey roses
speaking speaking
my Silk Socks music
speaking speaking

High Praise   the great

throat daring to fly perfect

More perfectly than a Star
                              would you dare
                    with your Sweet mind
            bloom my
      fate.

the dimension
or anything else
simple   say, leg   or   arm   or glass eye
My own Tooth Gold as Greek
Adonis   the Shout   for the trouble
of the raw vegetable
that you turn
your pretty head
against   what is a vegetable
Frightening a girl for
a Raw yam
from a guyanan Prince

Do you faythfully
see Myself   exult
ing like a
child who refuses

the Free Wind
answering
going anywhere

you Wonderful center of
My Mirth, Petruschka the
chicken in my comfort
able land

what if I increase
Taxes forever
Will Yezer strike
me down
the only crime
is my Zeal   in   this   house

I create tyme
YEARNING for you

my fat Kingly Woman

said KING LUGALANNEMUNDU

63

KING LUGALANNEMUNDU said

take a raw yam
the dimension   my plea   is   today
today is the dimension
answering my
fervor   today is   my feeling
I make today go anywhere
my plea
is my zeal
you fat Kingly woman
the chicken
is my comfort my
memory   the center of
My
mirth

I go Anywhere   hear my
tribal chant

it arranges the
COSMOS
the origins
today

the Laughter raw vegetables   is

Frightening us   its course is the center

e m b o d i m e n t
done most
unashamedly   the world

beginning again   unashamedly

by the Earth's Crust this
joye

XIV

LUGALANNEMUNDU / THE STORY TELLER
ALSO / THE SONG OF THE KING
AND / MAKE MY POEMS INTO PRAYERS,
SEZ KING LUGALANNEMUNDU

64

i'm a
Captain   in the African frontier
I Killed Walt Whitman   said king lugalannemundu

i investigated his
symple Heart
I witnessed his frustrating
the negroes
tomorrow and tomorrow and
tomorrow

would you like Volcanic
oyntment to rub on your
cherry lips, Demeter
Petruschka
the seed of my wisdom   I love

your breast-bones

133

today I will be
a child who refuses

to Disdain
the spyryt
or
the pretty heads
of
Harem Women
from Lybya   the first Lugalannemundu
copulated with a
thousand
Lybyan princesses
& bought
them   all windows   purple stained glass
to gaze from   all the day
they munched
chewing gum
From the west   they hada good
time

65

old Kid, with you
i Can keep my Nerve up
it's symple   i'm More than a thousand
white-men
with you
i have a sense of
Myself   i cannevah lose
arguments
even my Chewing baby lamb-eyes
is
innocent
my holy Vocal
concerto
loves this year
I met you
it's Very Symple
this Unyverse
tomorrow
you can
listen   to the same plant
saturate
the living artist's

body.   just a boy from
guyana in love with a
Housewife from a
SuperMarket   her coloured kerchief
articulating
the
arrangement
of the blood
I've Come
from a good
Class i love
the right ult
imate

the poplar wood So
Gracebearing
my own Shyness

66

THE SONG OF THE KING

                        my own Expectation
            i Could play with you
all day   face it, i can
            that i have a
        question
                            that digs   like inner
    peace

            talk, lose all
        the Arguments, i can
face that but
                        in the beginning Near the
        Soil in the afternoon when the
        Harmless worms begyn to frolic

                    a diamond of a true
            how lovely it was
    Dream   equal in terms of the
                                playing
            Worms

the living Exposure the red dye of your
                    soul
                    the covered rocks
            that are the presence of
        violence the algae
    measuring slow
                    the blue Soldiers of
            the Pasha
                        the red dye calling
        like blood
                    My life
    Human dissolved Sap

                              facing free &
                                backward
                        directly to a
                    purity
        Formed like ash,
                              hummed king lugalannemundu

king lugalannemundu

hummed   measuring slow   the beginning the

Sum

of the

Argument   a diamond of
blood

the face that

the guyanan winter

how lovely it was
formed from
poplar wood

the beginning the

Sum

of the

measuring slow   the humming of
his face

that

all day   slow   the lovely afternoon

backward
facing the Housewife
her coloured kerchief

symple

they both, sweet Chewing
baby lamb-eyes   talked
& he coming from a
good class a
symple prince
with Heavy
Purple lips
talked &

                    smoked tobacco
          she smiled
mad/ly

in the market centre
you compelled me to
Holiness   said Lugalannemundu
swaggering with his
imagination   the ruby rain
glinting
from the laughter of
KING   LUGALANNEMUNDU   just a boy with undeter-
mined
power just a boy
from the whirlwind
the Housewife's
Violet Eyes
re-shaping
a king's history & the whirlwind
stories
trembling from
his heart

sit near my body
across from
me
i am from
guyana &
you pass
my intestines
into the wild garden
of my Heart
my mouth is
for the
deluge   into the wild garden

of faire children starving,
that a goodly
King   will cherish
& feed

          my words   Petruschka
       I long for the fish
     bones that you
throw away
             I am Strengthened
                    by them

69

MAKE MY POEMS INTO PRAYERS / SEZ KING
LUGALANNEMUNDU

i am the Hermit Poet
singing to claude-levy

his symple opynyun
like 2 dogs to me
running all the way
down the road

doing it in the street
doing it in the street
like poetry
a white dog & a black dog

King Lugalannemundu
smirked.
Petruschka
my peppy Queen
my Roumanian gizzard
Rose of Salonika
think that I know not
where my next poem
is coming from

only look at me
with no warning
no warning
with Your Violet Eyes
it's better than whiskey
it's better than whiskey
Since so many
Hailing Fevers
I have known turning
a hundred times

                    embodying the generalized
              Anguish   i wish Only
         that the Poem
                    be good
         Spelling my
   Praise.

XV

THUS SPAKE PETRUSCHKA &
HER HEART TREMBLED

70

Understand Me
　　　　　　i Speak the Petruschka
you Beholde
　　　　　Lugalannemundu
　　hi, Old kid
　　　　　　　My Name is
　　　　Demeter
　　　　besides　　　what do I speak
　with a Kyng
　　　　　　I glimpse
　　　you feeding turtles
Eating Sunflower seeds　　　growing a
　　　　　　garden in faire
　　　　　guyana
　　　　　　　　With golden
　　　Buttons
　　　　　you allure me　　　Release
　　　　　　me of my Vows
with the old broom-maker
　　　　　　　you give me a
　　　　diamond of
　　　lips & Eyes
　　your first

step   to me   is with   your mythical

                    Laughter
                              I am your
                              fondest
                    Criminal Woman
      the Love /   sharpe   as earliest
                                                            Hope
                        the borne
            animal   of your   Swaggering
            &
      Shrewd
                dream.
                            King Lugalannemundu
                  Bending in the story
            of the old myths
                              cracking Sunflower
                  seeds like a lybyan
                  man who I give the
            bird to.

what else
do you want besides
Self-interest   the old myths or
Industrial cybernetics

New Jersey
where Yezer Smells the
landscape
give me a diamond
of Unconventional
Rhyming
like Dark Rum
/& I got a lotta Nerve
for
you.   I Am
Demeter Petruschka
with daisy
bows
even the Roumanian
Wolves step to me
In a dance
with idolatry
I am very Shy
as if dust crumbles
into organized Space & time
I manage
every hour   like a black-
Eyed woman
the mental image
my tooth
Ready for action
an evening meal
conveyed through space &
time
the passage
of Glass the quotations
of a Shark

Singing well &
bending in fayth
the condition
of a Vacant—
the rose family
Ocean.

once in Roumania

without a warning

a Criminal

Spelled my

Praise

by that story

the compelling

idol the

image of

the Vacant

Ocean the thick

ening circle   of   deliverance

the

Saga

of myself the brilliant

wheel plain

as heav'n

I

Petruschka of

a horse-dealer

wife of a

broom-maker   who

pitched woo & bullshitted

like a bohemian

lugalannemundu

a-man-o'nonsense

with a stubbed toe

bending in a new

Vindictive

dance

the Wolves of Roumania

bloodyminded & pass

ing   destruction   the twisting motion

of Anything

I without eyelids

re-shaped the skeleton
rays & light

the world again

                     playnly   say anything

      again the crust o' the

earth   Worsens

             i'm Frightened

        Said Petruschka Demeter the

        faces become windows that

    Still

          peculiarly

              the coiling spring

       of Anything

     that bubbles & yields

                & sinks to

          Old Age

        the illuminant

     shrill massacre   that boasts

          of

       Idiocy yu don't

            have to be

     Einstein

        to Map the ravages

of east to west

              i Petruschka revolve

        The Whole day

     against curses

    the rocks o' Yugoslavia

             the curses of

      Yezer   my weapon

       My string from heav'n

     hangin' springin' into

        the sacred

   fig tree

       the primal Nowhere

rays & light the burnished

           breath of the

                    morning the breath in
             the throat o'
         the believing
     King Lugalannemundu

Printed November 1978 in Santa Barbara & Ann
Arbor for the Black Sparrow Press by Mackintosh
and Young & Edwards Brothers Inc. Design by
Barbara Martin. This edition is published in paper
wrappers; there are 200 hardcover copies numbered
& signed by the author; & 26 copies have been
handbound in boards by Earle Gray and are lettered
& signed by the author.

Photo: Gerard Malanga

ROCHELLE OWENS, born April 2, 1936, is the
award-winning author of many controversial and innovative
plays and a pioneer in the experimental Off-Broadway
movement. Her plays have been performed throughout the
world and presented at festivals in Paris, Avignon, Berlin,
Edinburgh and Rome. *Futz* was made into a feature-length
film. She has published nine books of poetry, the most
recent being part of the series *The Joe Chronicles,* and two
collections of plays, *Futz and What Came After,* and *The
Karl Marx Play and others.* She has edited *Spontaneous
Combustion: Eight New American Plays.* A recipient of
Guggenheim, C.A.P.S., National Endowment for the Arts,
and the Yale School of Drama fellowships, her new play,
Emma Instigated Me, was developed during her residency
at The American Place Theatre as a Rockefeller Foundation
Playwriting Grantee. She is on the board of directors of the
Women's InterArt Center and now lives with her husband,
the poet George Economou, in New York City.